Hi, I'm Juantia Saint Louis.
I am a wife, mother of 3 adults, caregiver of our youngest, a friend, and supporter of many. Being that I have a life that requires me to wear many hats, self-care became a necessity. It can be so easy to lose oneself when you always put others before yourself. I know you feel me on that. The purpose of this ebook is for us, women to start normalizing self-care while supporting each other in our journey. Let's demystify why we all practice more self-neglect and cultivate more self-awareness through acts of self-care.

The Ultimate Guide for Women who are tired of being last on their to-do list.

<u>A Message from the Author:</u>

https://youtu.be/I_5pbBxe834

First, let me give you flowers for taking the 1st step on your journey to putting yourself on that continuous to-do list

Table of content

WHY IS

Self-Care

SO IMPORTANT

Yes, I know, it is tough to think about yourself but guess what?
It is the best way to take care of your family. Self-care should never be an option but a priority. Just like the announcement from the flight attendant over the intercom,

"Put your own oxygen mask on before assisting anyone else".

So often you are ripping and running, here, there, and everywhere on everyone else's agenda, burning the candle at both ends not realizing the major impact that it is taking on our mental & physical health, that you are not as important as everyone in your life.

Yes, you totally did this all wrong and it's not your fault. Generation after generation we all have been following in the footsteps of our overworked and unappreciated Mothers. You don't want to be that one that ends up sick, ill, or the unthinkable because you practiced self-neglect.

Statistically speaking, women will overlook all the signs that their body is giving them regardless of their personal cost. You have allowed yourself to live in the "You're ok", "Put your big girl panties on" or "pull yourself up by the bootstraps" society.

Your only guilt is not asking for help when you need it, yet instead, you will tell your spouse, significant other, or family, "I got it, thanks" with a fake smile. Knowing good and well you would appreciate a helping hand.

When you do accept the help, you feel guilty. but WHY?? Don't you deserve the help, the love, and the attention that you freely give to others ??

Women, in general, grow up with the assumption that they are the natural caregiver and if anyone lends you a hand you should be forever grateful.

It is time for you to train your mind that you are worthy of care, then start implementing self-care and accepting help. Being the caregiver doesn't give you the right to self-neglect. Your loved ones will begin to appreciate you more and there's no better time than now.

Self-Reflection

THE IMPORTANCE
OF
Affirmations

Have you ever tried affirmations? Affirmations are so important for you to reprogram your thinking. It encourages you to believe in certain things, to help you overcome self-sabotage and negative thoughts about yourself, situations, or circumstances.

As women, we all must realize that our children and family need us to be healthy for we are the glue that they can not live without. Stop applauding selflessness as if it is the best thing since sliced bread!! No Ma'am! Caring for yourselves less and less takes a toll on you mentally & physically as your health deteriorates. This is unacceptable!!

Women, motherhood can have many challenges in different stages that will test your patience, endurance, and the toughness of your skin. Some days you will feel like you have your Supermom cape on & can conquer, practically do it all, then some days you will feel like you need to crawl into bed and ball up.

Normalizing self-care will perhaps encourage other women to help themselves as much as they help their loved ones. Maybe motherhood would become less of a chore and more enjoyable when we all accept the love we should give ourselves. Fewer moms would feel less isolated, overwhelmed, and alone but become seen, heard and worthy.

Practicing affirmations is like having a reward system for your brain. Just like shopping at your favorite retail store and you get points for every $1 purchased. Your brain, fed positivity, learns how to deal more efficiently and less defensively. This will help you think more clearly and respond to others with respect and love.

By addressing the negative thought cycle at the root of the problem will help you recover quickly. Affirmations are a great tool to help you shift the balance as you replace the negativity with the positive. The best part is that you can use them in any situation.

So try this....

Repeat after me:

I am who God created me to be
I am worthy
I am loved
I am valuable
I am enough
I am choosing to love myself
I am beautiful
I am confident
I am the calm in the chaos
I am at peace
I am powerful
I am Mom, a great role model

You absolutely ARE!!!!

Self-Reflection

Fitness

YOU ARE NOT TOO BUSY!

Oh, man! It is tough to get started, listen, I know! Being the caregiver of your little ones, working in a corporate setting and family life, where do you fit it in???
Start small attainable workout goals for the week. Set your workouts in an app on your phone with reminders. When you start small you can not fail yourself or become disappointed.

Taking a walk alone, with a loved one or pet can do wonders for you mentally. It improves self-perception and self-esteem, mood, and sleep quality. It can also reduce stress, anxiety, and fatigue not to mention all the physical health benefits.

You will definitely begin to see the benefits of walking, to your mind and body so it should be a long-term investment to enhance your life.

As a Mom, we often use the excuse (yes, I said excuse) that we don't have time but what you really need to do is make time. It may take some practice but you can do it. Start early before your day gets away from you.

Join a gym for a small membership fee so you can change your environment from time to time. Some gyms have free classes you can take with your membership, adding a variety to your workout and keep it fun.

No time to get out? That's ok too, take an <u>online class</u>. It may be beneficial for you to do it early in the morning before your spouse leaves for work while children are still asleep. Make it a family affair, when your children are old enough to participate, have them tag along. Remember to keep it fun! Play a game of kickball, make a short obstacle course, go skating, take a family bike ride, or even just play tag in the backyard.
Endless Possibilities !!!

Being physical doesn't always have to be labeled as exercise but a fun activity. The key is to be active and moving. One of my favorite things to do after dinner is go for a walk, maybe it can be something the family does before bath and bedtime.

The long-term benefits will always outway any excuse that would keep you from taking care of yourself.

Self-Reflection

Mommy

TIME OUT

A must-have!!! Take yourself out and spend some quality alone time. Treat yourself to a budgeted pedicure once per month. Make this time where you can sit quietly, enjoy the massage and clear your head.

You will not have to spend money every time you take yourself out. Definitely plan it out so you are not stressed about the time you have to enjoy it without the rush to return home.

Get creative, go to a park, walk around or have a picnic by yourself. Enjoy nature by taking in a free outdoor concert. Don't want to go out, that's ok too.

Here are a few suggestions:

- Take a long hot bath
- Read a Book
- Update your playlist
- Do a Puzzle
- Listen to a <u>Podcast</u>
- <u>Journaling</u>
- Write down some goals
- Knit
- Do a Painting
- Gardening
- Crochet
- Paint your nails
- Take a Nap
- Plan your family vacation

Photo Credit
nURface Photography

Painting by theArtsy Empress

Self-Reflection

PERFECTING SAYING

no

You have to learn to let go. As a woman, wife, mom, and a good friend, you tend to take on more than you should. You don't need to do everything yourself, it's ok to let go and say no. I know you want to do everything right (your way) and be there whenever they need you but it could end up making you feel overwhelmed. Discouraged and the feeling of failure is not a good feeling. So let's not go there, let's focus on how you can change that thought pattern to command your time and perfecting saying No

Get yourself organized so you can start automating the things that can be. Your calendar will be your best friend in this particular task. Your time is valuable so make it easier on yourself.

Here are a few tips that may help you:

1. Meal Plan a week at a time
2. Add items to your grocery list as needed
3. Order your groceries online for pickup
4. Budget and automate your bills
5. Update your calendar often
6. Let someone else do it, when possible
7. Pencil yourself in!!!!

Regaining your time can definitely change your stress level because your time is being well managed so you can focus on what's important like family.

Making time for your loved ones can be motivating to be the best version of yourself. It is the perfect way to reduce stress and anxiety. Not only that, it can help you live a longer life, improve your mental health and increase your self-esteem.
It's ok not to participate in every outing you are invited to.

Family time can definitely be exactly what you need but it is up to you to create the time to connect.

Here are a few ideas that can help you gather your troop:

- Family Dinner
- Plan a monthly get together
- Read together
- Movie night
- Just sit and talk
- Go to the park/beach
- Game night

Remember life is too short not to put your time where it is needed the most! Just say no to the things that does not contribute to that.

Self-Reflection

PROTECT YOUR

Energy

Self-care is about your frame of mind for sure. So you protect your energy and focus on the positivity in your life.

We all know that life can throw curve balls left and right. You must continue to duck and dive all those punches of self-doubt, feeling less than and all the imperfections that want to disrupt your peace of mind.

Your energy will need to be protected so you can greet each day with a positive outlook, no matter what you are currently facing. Did you know people with a positive outlook have a one-third chance less likely to have a cardiovascular event 5-25 years than those who have a negative outlook??

Not only that, it can help keep your immune system strong. Nowadays we all need positive vibes all day long.

Hope and positivity help people make better health and life decisions and focus more on short & long-term goals.
You can always turn a negative thought or situation into a positive one by changing your frame of thought. Instead of stressing about the traffic in the early morning rush.

Focus on the extra time you get to jam to your favorite songs or extra time to say your morning affirmations.

Instead of focusing on the struggle of potty training your child, think about how much they have grown up and how many milestones they have accomplished without complications.

The best example: You are working on a project, you set daily goals for you to meet. Some days you may not meet those goals. So instead of focusing on what didn't get done, celebrate what you did accomplish and watch what this frame of mind does for you.

When you feel like you need some extra help to get your energy realigned, lean on family and friends.

The ones that are always encouraging and supporting you from near or far, over the phone or through text. The ones that will have you laughing within the five minutes into the conversation, yea them! They know your situation and are ready to go to bat on your behalf to lift your spirit. You are not alone!

I know this is a lot to take in but you are worth every moment that you can hone in on that positive energy.

Just imagine for a minute, close your eyes, see yourself soaking in a hot bath with your favorite essential oils, lots of bubbles, and candles all around. While you are in there breathe in all the positivity and exhale all the negative.

Self-Reflection

PRIORITIZE, PRIORITIZE

Prioritize

Make yourself a priority!! If you pencil yourself in as I mentioned, stick with it as if it was any other appointment that you could not miss. At this time you would have already scheduled childcare with a sitter, spouse, or family member. You have decided exactly what you wanted to do and or where you decided to go if anywhere at all but a different room in the house.

It's your appointment and prep is needed so you can enjoy the fullness of your time.
Now this time does not include your annual appointment with a doctor, which is also a priority.
This will be separate from all womanly appointments, which is also self-care but don't short yourself.
No, your children's doctor's appointments don't count either, nice try.
This is about you, if you choose to include your family, that's ok but remember to do something just for you. Alone time is a time for reflection, self-love, and refocus.

Don't make it hard to treat yourself no matter how small of a time you start at. Your family will not always understand your absence but will appreciate your return when they see what it has done for you. It is ok to say yes to rest, if you don't find the time your body will choose a time for you. At that point, it may take you longer to recover.

You may think your needs may not matter, you feel unworthy because that was all you saw growing up.

Communicating your needs to others as to why you need to honor your appointment with yourself can be hard. It is up to you to see your worth, submit and honor yourself.

You can't just self-care your way out of burnout. You need to work on your mindset. Challenge the thoughts that your needs don't matter, use your affirmations and positive thinking and reverse it.

Still stuck on what to do, again start small. Here are some more ideas that may help you get started:

1.   Write your affirmations
2.   Do some journaling
3.   Spend some time outdoors
4.   Treat yourself to some coffee/tea
5.   Go to the library
6.   Enjoy your couch
7.   Go bike riding
8.   Take your skates for a spin
9.   Scream your head off on a rollercoaster ride
10.   Go to a concert

Self-Reflection

THE JUGGLING ACT:

Family!

There are so many things you juggle to keep everything on point for your family. You have to keep the day-to-day routines for the family, your work life and keep the money in order which can leave you feeling overstretched and overwhelmed. Is this why self-care is at the bottom of your list?
No sis, it should definitely be the reason why it is at the top.

Mom, Mom, Mom is a constant calling you know all too well. Annoying as it can be, you always muster up a way to acknowledge your children and get things done.

They will drive you up a wall if you let them, take your sanity and power back. No need to feel guilty and/or apologetic, not everything that they want needs your special attention.

The importance of leaving your family to regroup will end up being very beneficial for them. You want to be calm as a cucumber when they are beckoning, so give yourself permission.

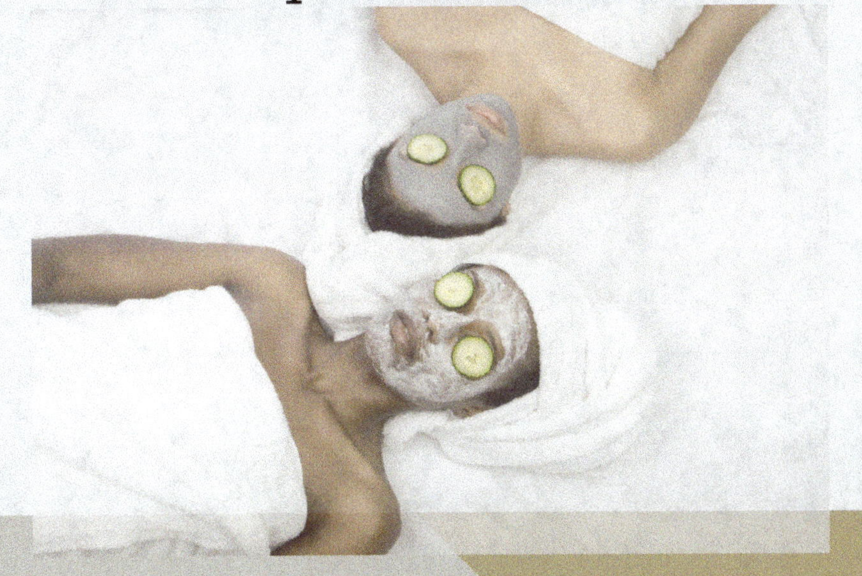

Self-Reflection

Work Life

Some of you may work in the field, work from home, or searching for a job or business opportunity.

Your job or business will have its own set of demands on you. You may feel guilty because your job is taking a lot of your time and energy that you so desperately need for your family.

Not to mention you may bring the work home to complete because of the demand. It can be hard to balance at times and when you finally get that week off for vacation, you can't rest because you feel like you have to make up for a lost time.

You are not alone! According to CNBC, there are 35 million working moms and 42% of women are suffering from workplace burnout. This is huge! I truly don't want you to be a part of this statistic.

On top of work demands, you have been stressing about finding affordable and safe childcare. During the Pandemic, most of you had no choice but to reduce your hours, work from home at a reduced pay rate, and practically homeschool your children. You definitely had your Supermom cape on then. I applaud you for pressing through but you must take some time back for yourself.

Your world can survive without you from time to time so you can refresh. You must always keep in mind that your children are watching, do you want them to experience or practice self-neglect like what you are doing to yourself? I think not! Life is too short to be stretched so thin.

Self-Reflection

THE JUGGLING ACT:
Money!

When it comes to your finances, you may tend to shy away from treating yourself, especially with growing children who are always in need of a new pair of sneakers or something from a new surprise school supply list.

Having security about finances is part of self-care. Peace of mind that you can provide whatever your children may need and when they need it is essential to your mental health.

Often people tend to think that the man of the household is always the provider in many ways but it's the woman behind the scenes that is calculating the cost and paying the bills.

Seeing and not having enough can create a major barrier for you to perform your parental duties at your full capacity. It can cause depression and a dysfunctional family. Your stress does affect your children, no matter how hard you try to hide it.

When your household is overstretched and in need of something extra without the sacrifice of taking even more time away from home, you have options.

Having a small business from home can not only bring you more income but help you reclaim some of the money that is going out.

You can absolutely make it a family thing, hire your own children. Doing so will give you more time with your family as you come together to meet a business goal or complete a business project and make the extra income you need for a family vacation, for your Mommy time out and things your children need outside of the essentials.

52% of Small businesses are home-based. Many have a low investment to get started and are a business in a box. The flexibility alone is worth giving it a shot to regain your time, freedom, and peace of mind.

Find out more & contact me

What you putting in your temple

Being healthy is definitely geared in the right direction toward selfcare. Are you truly listening to your body? I know it's a little tough to pinpoint everything your body needs but guess what you won't know all of it at once and it's ok. Just like any other thing in life, it will take time. So give yourself some grace and patience.

Nourishing your body with the right foods can make a huge difference in your health, help fight fatigue and even protect you from chronic noncommunicable diseases.

Start slow if you have to, add something healthier on your plate 1-2 times a day. Let your body and taste buds adjust to increase tolerance for it. You can do it!!
Starting to include lean protein, vegetables, and nuts in the diet every day can help you stay healthy and prevent certain chronic conditions.
Some plant foods, such as cruciferous vegetables (i.e broccoli cabbage, or cauliflower) and berries, contain particularly beneficial compounds, including polyphenols and glucosinolates
(<u>for your gut health</u>).

Incorporating these foods into your weekly meal plan, try a 2-week rotation. It can help to ensure you get a wide variety of beneficial nutrients. It also prevents you from having a repetitive diet and can be more satisfying and appealing. You don't want to become bored and quit your new eating habit.

A healthier version of yourself is waiting, just stick to it and give yourself time. You should remember that having an occasional treat is not going to be harmful to overall health, as long as they ensure a regular and varied intake of nutrients. Please consult your physician for personalized medical advice.

(This content is for informational and
educational purposes only)

Self-Reflection

JUST

Breathe

SIS

You are your toughest critic, you constantly beat yourself up with negative thinking and self-sabotage verbiage that you can live your life without. Retraining your mind to focus on the positivity that you so desperately need is an absolute must!

Life is challenging enough without the naysayer in the back of your mind that keeps you from treating yourself well. It keeps you from moving forward in your goals, it keeps your mind clouded and takes a toll on your body from the lack of rest. Just Breathe Sis!

Lean on God for everything! The negativity will steal, kill and destroy the joy that has been instilled within you since birth. Love, happiness, and peace will find you when you become content with whom you were created to be. Regular self-care practices will help you get back to the balance you seek.

Then and only then you can begin to appreciate the precious gift of parenthood. Watch your children grow and blossom, mimicking the qualities that you exude from that happy place you have found from within. You have a huge responsibility but that doesn't mean you have to lose yourself in the process. Baring, caring, and loving your children doesn't make you any less significant. You have been blessed with a great gift to nurture.

Let's normalize celebrating your efforts in taking care of yourself vs neglecting yourself. You Matter!! You were not created to stress, worry or treat yourself like the welcome mat outside of your front door for everyone to walk on and dust their feet. No Ma'am!

Pick your head up, wipe your tears, put your shoulders back and reflect on the things you like about yourself. Start there. Take it one day at a time, walking on the path you see yourself on.

The path of I am enough, I am important, I am strong, I can do all things through Christ who strengthens me, I am a conqueror, I am loved, I am at peace and I am a child of God. The person you were created to be. Never give up on you, your little ones are watching like a hawk. If you don't see what

you are doing is for them, then don't do it!! Show them how to value themselves, show them how it's ok to have quiet time, show them that self-care is vital for a well-rounded person. Action speaks louder than words, right? Remember you are a pillar in your family, part of the foundation that must not crumble or fall. So take care of yourself and practice some form of self-care each day, you are worth it!
So Just Breathe Sis !!

If you haven't already joined, the Community of Women & Mothers encourages each other and shares self-care routines, tips, and tricks that will ease the everyday hustle called life. Let's celebrate each other and normalize self-care.

<u>Join the movement</u>
Contact me

Self-Reflection

RESOURCE PAGE:

TRAINING AND FITNESS

HTTPS://JHAMPTONHEALTH.COM/THANK-YOU-SALES-PAGE-LONG1631470872763

NUTRITIONAL AID

HTTPS://RETAIL.TOTALLIFECHANGES.COM/KNOWYOURWEALTH

SELF CARE MENTORSHIP

HTTPS://MINDESCAPEVIBE.COM/

PODCAST

HTTPS://WWW.BLOGTALKRADIO.COM/SUCCESSWITHNICOLA

PLANNER

HTTPS://PINKMILLIONAIRECLUB.COM/POWER-MOVES-PLANNER/

Thank you!

Submit your Book review